DRAWING THE LINE

North American Edition © 2015 Ad Astra Comix
Ontario, Canada
adastracomix@gmail.com | www.adastracomix.com

First published in 2015 by Zubaan Books Pvt. Ltd.,
128b Shahpur Jat, First Floor,
New Delhi 110049, India
Email: contact@zubaanbooks.com
Web: www.zubaanbooks.com

In partnership with Goethe-Institut/Max Mueller Bhavan New Delhi

ISBN 978-0-9940507-1-7

Designed by Anita Roy (1st Ed. www.anitaroy.net), and Nicole Marie Burton (2nd Ed.)
Cover design by Priya Kuriyan (1st Ed.) and Nicole Marie Burton (2nd Ed.)
Printed by Marquis Printing, Quebec: www.marquisbook.com

Ad Astra Comix is an independent community hub for comics with social justice themes. Based in Ontario, Canada and operating across North America, Ad Astra Comix produces, promotes, publishes, and offers consultation and curatorial advice regarding comics that seek to amplify marginalized voices and dismantle oppressive frameworks. In addition to our regular website, we are on Facebook, Twitter, Instagram, Pinterest, and Tumblr.
www.adastracomix.com

Zubaan is an independent feminist publishing house based in New Delhi with a strong academic and general list. It was set up as an imprint of India's first feminist publishing house, Kali for Women, and carries forward Kali's tradition of publishing world-quality books to high editorial and production standards. Zubaan means tongue, voice, language, in Hindustani. Zubaan publishes work in the areas of the humanities, social sciences, as well as in fiction, general non-fiction, and books for children and young adults under its Young Zubaan imprint.
www.zubaanbooks.com

Drawing the LINE

INDIAN WOMEN FIGHT BACK!

North American Edition

edited by
Priya Kuriyan, Larissa Bertonasco
Ludmilla Bartscht, and Nicole Marie Burton

zubaan

CONTENTS

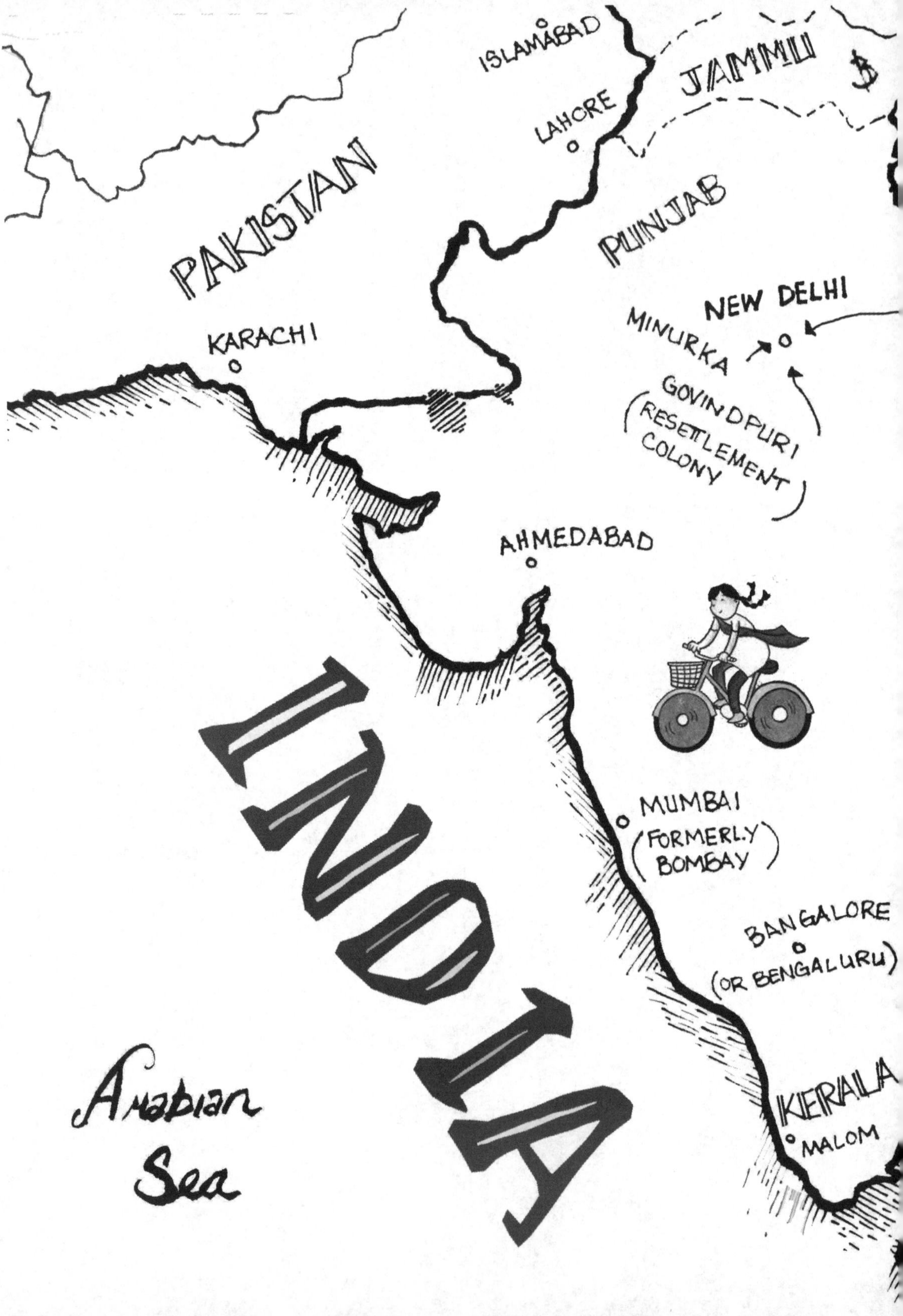
ISLAMABAD
JAMMU
LAHORE
PAKISTAN
PUNJAB
NEW DELHI
MINURKA
GOVINDPURI
(RESETTLEMENT
COLONY)
KARACHI
AHMEDABAD
INDIA
MUMBAI
(FORMERLY
BOMBAY)
BANGALORE
(OR BENGALURU)
Arabian
Sea
KERALA
MALOM

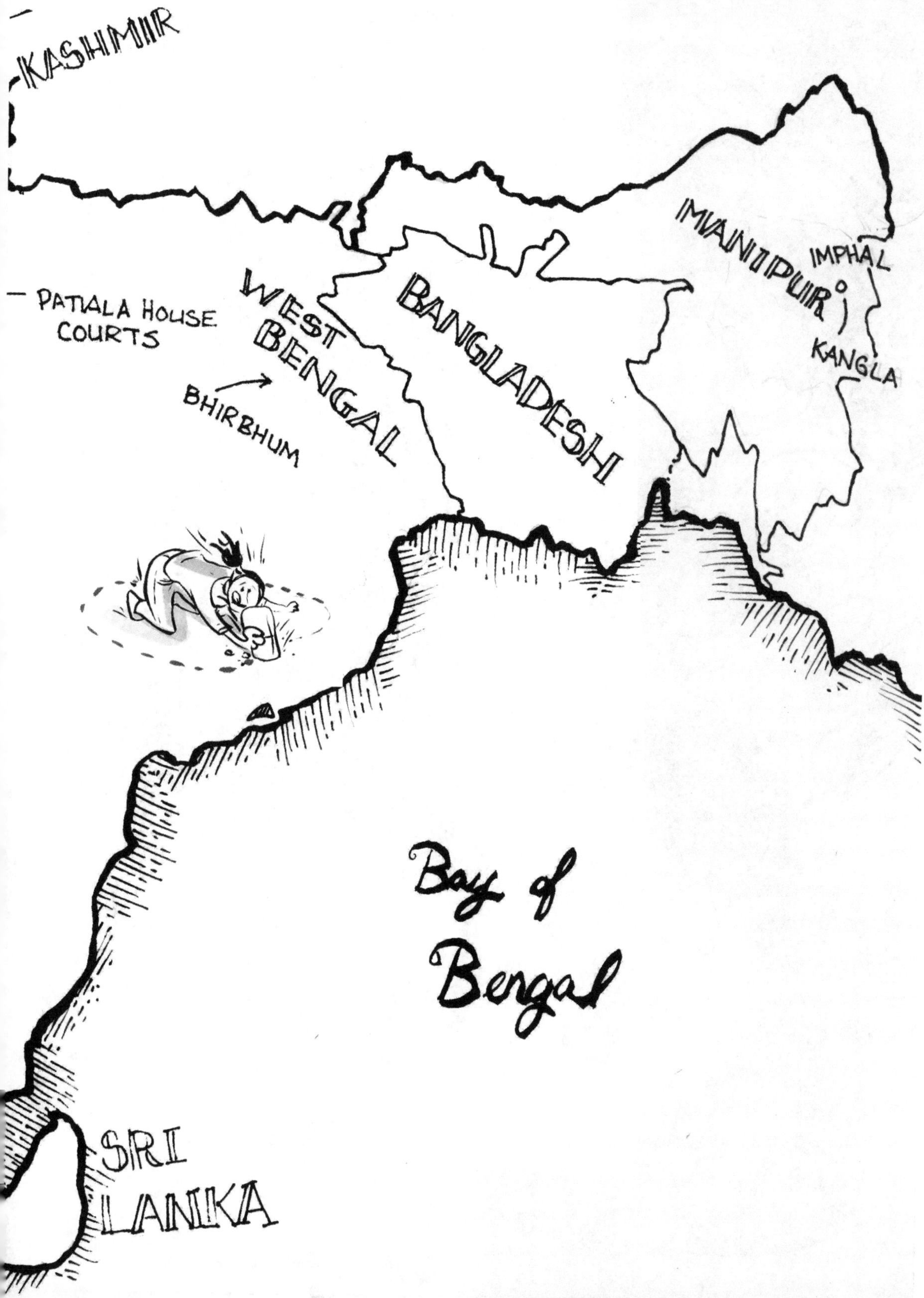
KASHMIR
PATIALA HOUSE COURTS
WEST BENGAL
BHIRBHUM
BANGLADESH
MANIPUR
IMPHAL
KANGLA
Bay of Bengal
SRI LANKA

BY soni satpathy-singh

FOREWORD

There was a period of time in my life where I would sketch and write alternative narratives of Hindu mythology. In my recreations, Sita would require that Rama also enter Agni to prove his loyalty and purity. Sita's worth wouldn't always be trifled with and tested.

She might suggest Rama seek counseling. Maybe she'd live alone in a modest cottage where she could pen a tell-all memoir of her life and times in consortship with the heir apparent; and how his leadership cemented institutionalized sexism. She might even take up archery as a hobby.

At any rate, the last thing she'd do is retreat back into the womb of the Earth because it was the only escape from the maddening contempt society held for her and other women. No, in my version, things would be different. Sita would speak out, she would use her divinity to buck the system. In my version, she'd stick around and make sure people understood their perpetuation of gender violence.

Well, my version is just that: my version, steeped in a bunch of what ifs and fantasy. I do wonder how different society would be if these particular stories and lore hadn't been passed down from generation to generation as Truth. I wonder where we'd be today if the notion of an ideal woman wasn't so intricately tied to martyrdom and servitude and the idea that a woman, the ideal woman, must sacrifice her Self for some greater good, the greater good usually meaning the progress of man.

But we can't recreate mythology and history though, can we? The prevailing version of lore and tradition carries with it a subset of microaggressions so deeply embedded in culture that bucking the system can sometimes feel moot. But then, projects like Drawing the Line emerge and I remember I don't need to recreate stories of the supposed "divine." The power is in the profane, in the everyday, in real women and in our narratives.

Drawing the Line nudged me to remember why I had taken up creating comics to begin with. I wanted--no, scratch that, I needed to create and foster alternative narratives, because acknowledging sexism, thinking through it, exploring how it affects us as individuals and as a group are powerful tools for activism.

Reading the narratives of these women and being moved by their accounts made my being asked to write this foreword all the more electric. I felt I was witnessing the phenomena of butterfly wings aflutter. Butterflies, you ask?

The butterfly effect has been cited as a metaphor for social change in both feminist literature and academia. Political scientist Robin L. Teske explains it to be a part of chaos theory, a theory that maintains that systems are sensitive to miniscule changes. Imagine then that a butterfly flaps its wings in one part of the world. A seemingly trivial gesture, no? No.

All those little flaps are believed to exert a pressure on surrounding air molecules that then cause bigger, atmospheric events to occur in other parts of the world. Or as Teske explains, "small differences in initial conditions can create big differences in final outcomes." Do you see where I'm going with this?

Drawing the Line is exerting that pressure, creating a ripple effect and change well outside the borders of India. It is a powerful path to intersectional feminism.

In this day and age of media sensationalism, what we miss—and what Drawing the Line unapologetically captures-- are the microaggressions of the everyday, the "stuff" that is not headline worthy as it is not necessarily eventful. But it is real, nonetheless.

They are the constant messages, subliminal or otherwise, which suggest that our self-worth is contingent upon, say, our skin color, our entering into a marriage, the dowry we bring, the cat-calls we must endure, and the gender violence that has become so commonplace that humanity no longer bats an eye; and so Drawing the Line flaps a wing... fourteen, to be precise. In bringing these microaggressions to light and grounding them in the context of real narratives by real Indian women, I am given the opportunity to better understand a culture from where I came from but in which I no longer live.

Projects such as Drawing the Line are vital pieces of work for those of us who are feminists in the diaspora because, as we sometimes find ourselves straddling two cultures, it is easy to become susceptible to the sensationalism of western media and to use western metrics to gauge progress in India. Drawing the Line does away with all that and gives direct "from the ground" accounts of narratives, sans media spin and white washing. These Indian women aren't looking to anyone else to voice their narratives. On top of that, they are using a graphic novel—an art medium dominated by men—as an amplification of their voices. The flutter!

I would like to think that in voicing the sexism, the shadeism, the classism, all the atrocious -isms intertwined with gender violence, these women did what even the ideal woman, Sita, couldn't do. They didn't retreat into the ground. Rather, they stood their ground. They're breaking new ground. They remind me that you don't have to be the ideal woman to make an impact. In fact, it's precisely when we choose not to be the ideal woman that we truly chip away at the patriarchal constructs that kept our foremothers contained.

No more. We're drawing the line.

SONI SATPATHY-SINGH

Soni Satpathy-Singh is the creator and artist of SketchyDesi.com, a website that provides original comics and articles for the South Asian Diaspora.

HARiNi KANNAN

When a baby girl is born — especially in a South Indian family — the most important question is whether she is dark-skinned or fair. Her complexion is directly linked to how much dowry the family will have to give in order to get her married. In my story, the mother has gone through a lot in her own life, due to her complexion, and doesn't want her daughter to suffer the same fate. The baby, however, has her own ideas about the matter!

I began my foray into the field as a cartoonist and amateur caricaturist, but was drawn towards bright colours, quick wit, humour and charm of illustration and graphic design.

I now spend my free time watching washing machines swirling comfortingly and walking into street lamps, waiting for inspiration to strike. Or maybe lightning!

www.behance.net/harinikannan2491

THAT'S NOT FAIR

•HARINI KANNAN•

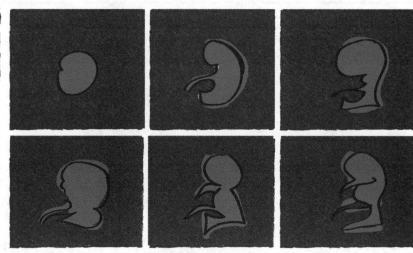

Somewhere in a shady clinic ...

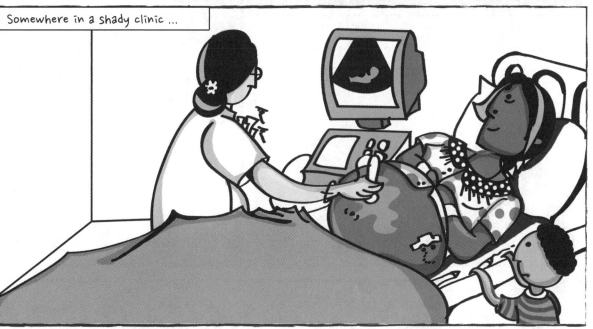

It's a girl!

Oh!

IS YOUR DAUGHTER NOT MARRIED **YET!!**

CALL
1800-040-8765

GLUG! GLUG!.. GLUG

Ma!! I'm just getting fat! Good luck with getting me out!

In India, being dark is certainly not as asset. In order to avoid dowry, women take countless measures to lighten their complexion. In this case, even an unborn child is not spared.

Do not!!

You should!

You can't!!

Maybe you can...

@#%$&^*(*%

Statistics show that dark children are...

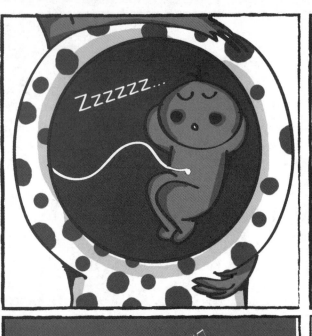

The ninth month...

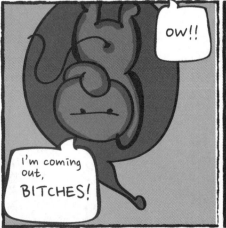

* Tamil lullaby

DiTi
MiSTRY

I'm 5 feet 2 inches tall, petite and skinny. Growing up in Delhi, the idea of dealing with the crowds on a Mumbai train had always been a nightmare. Until I did it!

I moved to Mumbai four years ago for my graduation. It was hard at first, till the everyday adventure of travelling in a 'local' became a part of life. It was then that I realised how integral these local trains are to the city and to the millions of commuters who use them.

In order to get under the skin of the city you need to take a ride in a Mumbai local. It opens your eyes to the hardship and determination of people. Never one for the hustle and bustle, it took me time to adjust. But it soon dawned on me that I wasn't a visitor anymore.

You see, I'm a person who loves to find stories and emotions behind every face. I love to doodle their complex identities, their expressions and emotions, portraying them through my eyes.

I visualized the Ladies' compartment as a being in itself, with a certain energy that was quite different from all the other compartments of the train. The women passengers are so animated! I wanted to capture some of this energy in my drawings for this story.

Hearing stories about Mumbai and coming face to face with the city turned out to be very different. I was lost, and was not sure if I ever wanted to be part of it.

I meekly followed orders and removed and shook out my clothes in a private cabana, held together by women I didn't know.

It took an incident like this to make me realise I was actually a part of this sisterhood of daily commuters and not just an observer of their lives. They had accepted me as one of their own long before I knew it.

Suddenly, I knew I wanted to belong...

RESHU SINGH

I am an illustrator and artist working in New Delhi. I studied Applied Art at College of Art, New Delhi and graduated in 2012. The idea of the story was born out of observing the general restlessness that develops within a home when a child reaches marriageable age.

'The Photo' is the story of a girl named Bena who doesn't want to get married while everyone in her family has a different take on it. But more than that, it's about Bena facing her fear of losing her 'true' self.

The story is a study of the idea of identity and of our expectations of ourselves and each other.

www.reshusingh.com

Wouldn't mind another cup of tea...

Lose the paper first then!

Mom did her 'Master's' in economics, and she used to paint landscapes.

Once she painted a pair of tigers – size of the real ones.

Bena! Make tea for papa. Will you have a cup?

No.

What should I make for dinner?

I don't know. Pulao?

But since she has to babysit the three of us, she doesn't get to do any of the fun stuff.

I don't need taking care of!

But, of course. You don't even wash your own clothes!

I choose not to. I know how to wash clothes. We have a freaking machine to wash clothes, Mumma!

Will get a machine to raise a family?

I already have a family. I want to live with you and take care of you all.

You have no idea what you are talking about. You're too naive, don't even know your own good.

Everyone knows their own good.

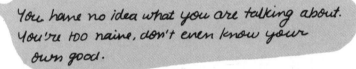

And their own fear.

You gave up everything to become a superhero to us.

But collected so much bitterness along the way...

Isn't being happy heroic too?

SOUMYA MENON

I rediscovered the Ideal Boy posters when I started collecting them during my student days. The posters — or 'educational charts' as they were called — along with matchbox labels and old film posters, added to my growing hoard of Found Objects.

In their all-too-familiar textbook illustration style, their garish colours and warped perspective, I found an Even More Warped perspective: the girls in all these posters were forever depicted doing some kind of chore in the background: cooking, cleaning and dutifully serving the Ideal Boy.

This graphic narrative is an attempt at
turning things around. A between-the-panels exploration of some of these preset notions of the Ideal Girl. I wanted the Ideal Girl to tell her own story. One in which she is set free.

I am an animation filmmaker and illustrator.
I like to travel often, and try my hand at other occupations like painting walls.

scrambled-scribbles.blogspot.in

AN IDEAL GIRL

— SOUMYA MENON

The Ideal Boy is well educated and cultured.

The Ideal Girl was well educated, of course.

Yet they encouraged her to pursue her hobby.

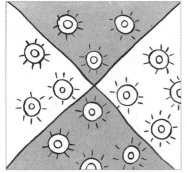

Not as an art, though.

Or even a skill.

But just a role, like any other.

For tradition decreed

this was the prospective bride's way of earning her dowry.

The Ideal Girl is well educated and cultured, too.

The Ideal Boy is well settled.

The Ideal Girl

juggled her household,

family,

and job very well

without any help from Ideal Boy

who showed up

from time to time

to take away her earnings

making her wish he stayed away

for good. She could certainly do without him.

The Ideal Girl is very well settled.

An Ideal Boy respects family.

The Ideal Girl studied well.

So well she was accepted into one of the country's best universities.

Yet she was told

that she had to think of her brother,

the Ideal Boy

who would soon be applying to university.

Two university courses was too much expenditure.

Of course, she should study,

at a local college perhaps,

and be a good sister.

An Ideal Girl, too, respects family.

An Ideal Boy protects his sisters.

Ideal Boy decided to prevent crime

and protect girls.

And so the girl commuting in the city

who disappeared

into thin air

was the girl who became another statistic

that reinforced the diktat

to protect girls

by ensuring they were home by nightfall

or better still, that they stayed put at home.

An Ideal Girl is protected by her Brothers.

Ideal Boys don't complain.

When Ideal Girl

asked Ideal Boy

to share the household chores,

they were all surprised!

Even shocked!

For Ideal Girl was not in the habit

of talking back

to her elders.

In fact, she was not in the habit

of talking at all.

Ideal Girls don't complain, either.

The Ideal Girl walked long distances every day

to get to work.

They told her that there was no need for her to work.

She refused.

They asked her to find work closer home.

She said that she liked what she was doing.

They got her a bicycle

so that she could get back home sooner.

Instead, she cycled

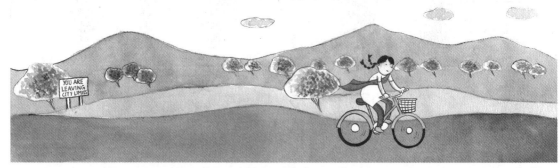

further and further away. She decided she had had quite enough of being the Ideal Girl.

PRIYANKA KUMAR

This story is primarily an afternoon story, born out of memories of tea, post-school sunlight and 'Enter The Dragon' dubbed in Tamil playing on television, my grandmother offering an exultant fist-pump every time something explosive and magic happened onscreen.

Also contained in it are images I remember of several living rooms. All of them were similar in one way or another, but populated by warm, wise, interesting women who were experts at improvisation — stories, scandals, recipes, cushion covers, nothing escaped embellishment. Their worlds almost outshone the ones my friends and I made up on a regular basis.

Now that I am trying to live a grown-up life, I find that chores get done easier when you are thinking of entirely different things altogether.

Drawing this made me dwell upon more things than I'd bargained for — boredom, loneliness, the art of being preoccupied, and the various ways we attempt to escape the everyday spaces we inhabit.
Besides, you know, who doesn't like monsters and tentacles?

I like fiction, tea, paint and stories with open endings, but you probably know that by now...

priyanka-kumar.blogspot.in

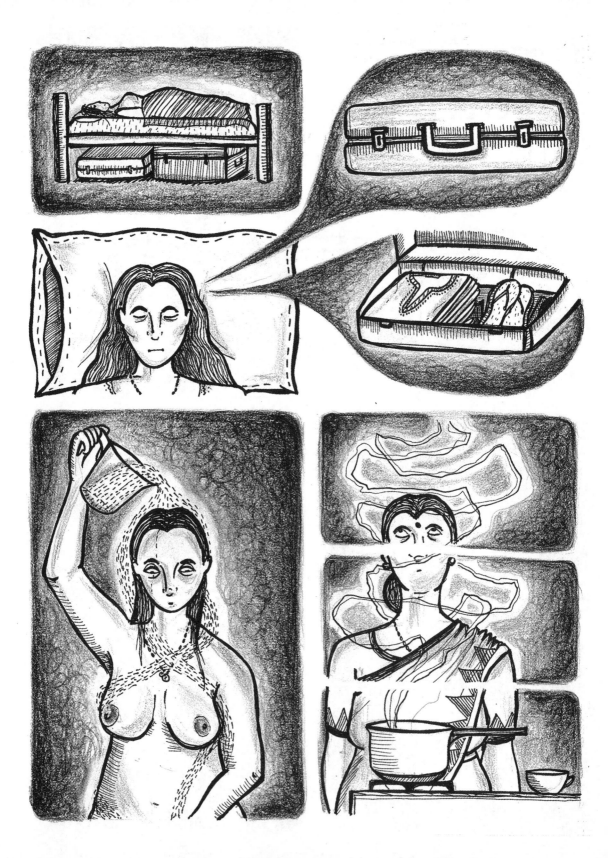

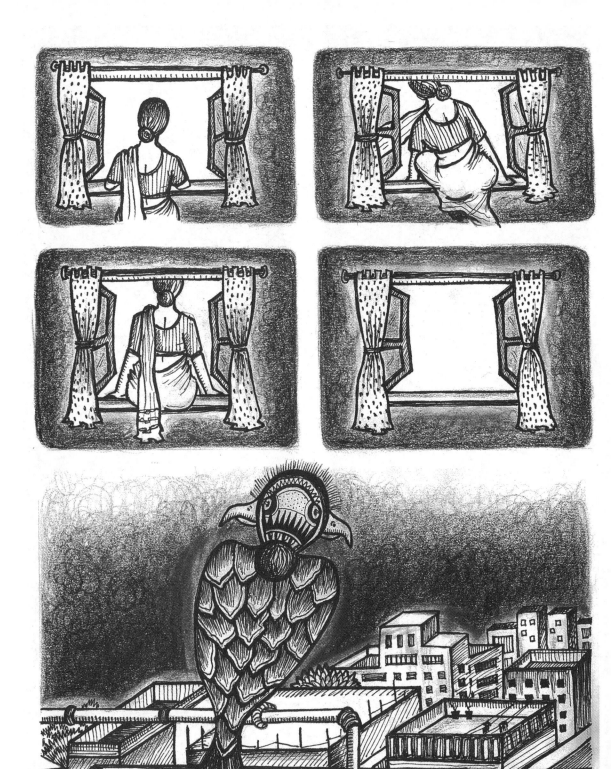

NEELIMA P
ARYAN

While looking for a story about gender, I went to my mother asking for a story. She said she has a simple story and read it out to me.

My mother leads an alternate life on the blogosphere. She writes in Malayalam — poetry, short stories and sometimes travelogues.

There is no utopia in the virtual world either. It is ridden with sexism. My mother explained that there was a discussion on what women's writing is, and that categorizing any writing as such is to pigeonhole it, and in some sense to ignore the quality or the sizeable amount of literature written by women. This story, originally titled *Pennezhuthu* ('A Woman's Writing'), was written in response to one such discussion and published on her blog at marunadan-prayan.blogspot.com.

The challenge when illustrating an existing story that uses beautiful language and a distinct dialect is to express that which is lost in translation and transliteration. To avoid that, this story was imagined as a silent story with speech only in the last frame. The story is set in rural Kerala and in its simplicity conveys the unpredictability of nature.

Neelima is a queer feminist, shies away from being called an artist but is known to art away in the virtual world. Her work is not for the light-hearted or the narrow-minded for it is mostly loud, and about women, large bodies and queer love.

Facebook.com/NiloferBLUink

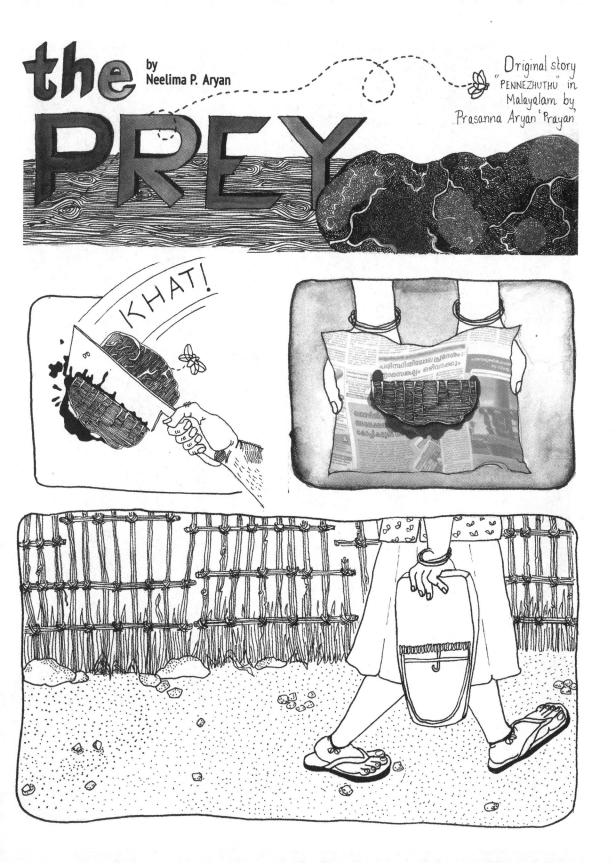

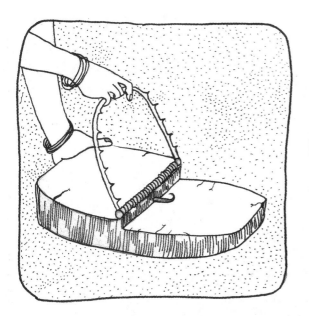

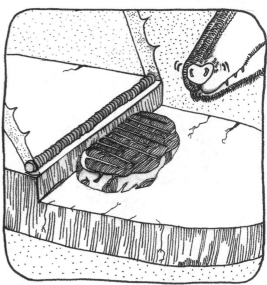

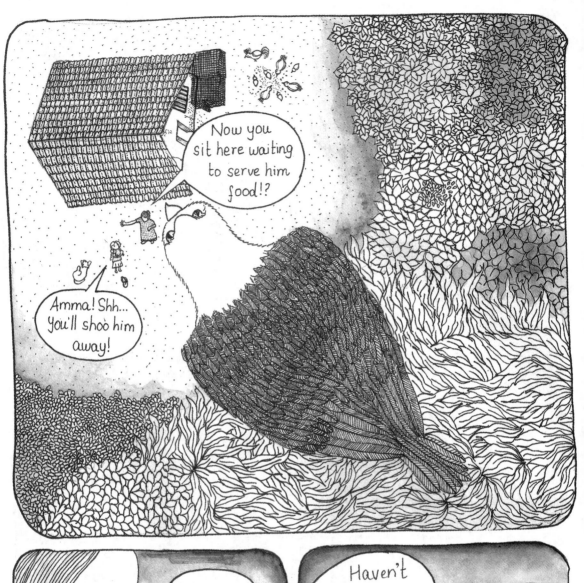

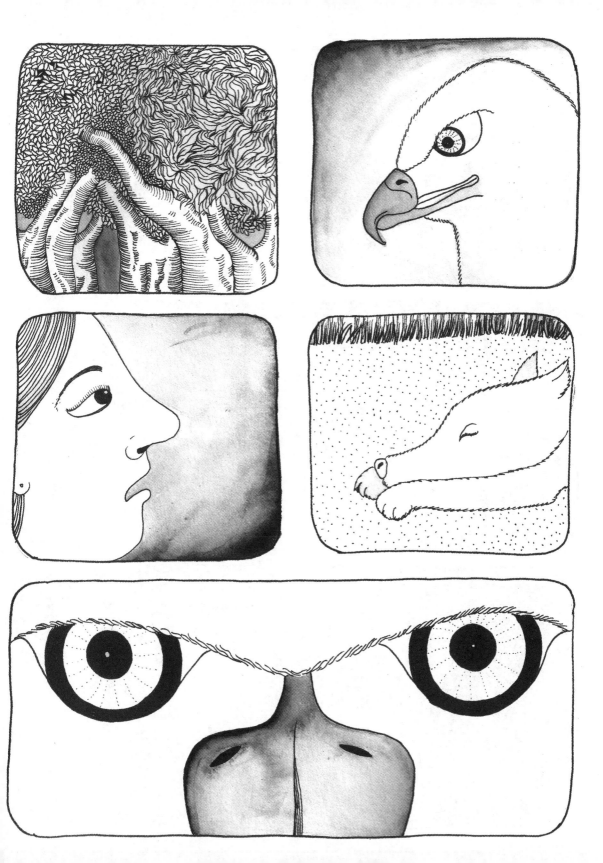

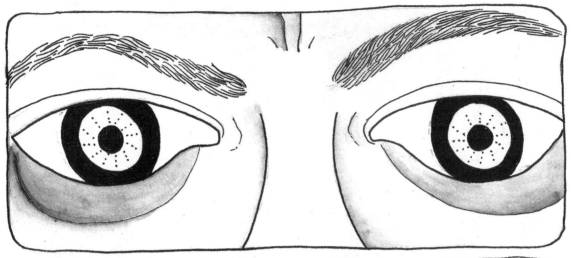

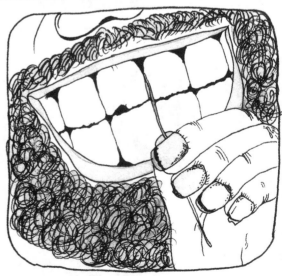

BHAVANA SINGH

The odd inner life of a pigment is not easy to express, but my absolute despair and bewilderment at the absurdity of human desires helped. Of course, 'fairness' and beauty are at the visible spectrum of difficulties we concoct for ourselves, and the many standards we judge ourselves by simply boggle the mind.

I'm just really glad to learn that I can actually 'draw' and will continue illustrating.

INNER Beauty AND melanin

by B.S.R.

*Some 'fairness' products are packaged with free shade cards to help users see their skin transform over the course of time — a handy, little scale of self-loathing. In the same spirit of public service, the standard ad copy for most beauty products pairs 'dark' with other simple words like 'anti-', 'dead', 'dull' or 'damaged' to aid consumer understanding. Some avoid using 'dark' altogether, so as to enhance consumer clarity by keeping the focus on 'fairness' and 'whiteness'. Care is also taken to avoid using models with skin tones darker than acceptable levels in order to protect sensitive viewers from the adverse effects of reality.

And while significant scientific studies have been unable to prove that 'dark/-er skin' is, by itself, a disease, a deficiency or a danger to general well-being, advertising has made pioneering advancements in this field. Marketeers are aware that in many cases dark skin has been seen to cause social and psychological difficulties to the wearers and/or observers, but because topical creams and lotions to reduce human intolerance, insecurity and discrimination are yet to be developed, they have tried to meet this challenge with an effective alternative.

melanin

IN MORPHOSIS

melanin
IN
SKINTERESTING
FACTS

THIS LITTLE PIGMENT
ALONE ACCOUNTS FOR
A BUSINESS WORTH
₹ 3,000 CRORES
ANNUALLY IN INDIA.
- *The Economic Times,*
April 14, 2014

An estimated 298 tonnes*
of skin-whitening products
are sold annually in the country.
This is in addition to other
services and treatments that
offer to — WHITEN/LIGHTEN/
BRIGHTEN/TIGHTEN/BLEACH/
DEPIGMENT/DETOXIFY/RESURFACE/
EXFOLIATE/HYDRATE/REJUVENATE/
PEEL/POLISH; make skin GLOW/
FAIRER/SMOOTHER/FRESHER/
CLEANER/CLEARER/SOFTER/
SUPPLER/SPOTLESS/FLAWLESS/
YOUNGER-LOOKING,
all naturally
and from
deep within.

* Bloomberg
Businessweek,
Dec 5, 2013

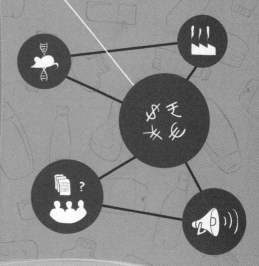

Now with **FREE** TRIVIA!

How much has the Odisha
state government planned to
spend on healthcare (in crores)
in the next three years?*
A. 30
B. 300
C. 3,000

*Ans. C (as reported by The New Indian Express, Jan 11, 2014)

melanin
in Silent
JUDGEMENT

click..
..click

Wow!
Is that the
phot... हााय!
I'm looking
soo fat!

But check
her out!

They all look
the same,
yaa!

81 likes?!
Seriously!

click..
82!

No. 1

Supermel & YOOVYJI

featuring OOBTAN™

IN ENTITLEMENT

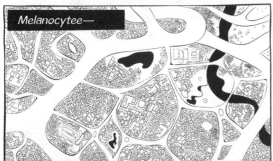

Melanocytee—

For some, it's a tense Thursday at work, in this big, bustling metropolis.

home to a million hopes.

Meanwhile for others...

BZZT CRACKLE

M! DO YOU COPY? M!

Hyper-Elmsg activity detected in sector 17!

HOP TO IT!

You'll also need to send in that invoice today!

Uh...and turn in the gear after

BZ2T

CRASH

⊕#!

ZIP

OW

♪ ♫

Even as other simple citizens remain entirely indifferent to imminent danger.

But Supermel is on the job!

After a short break!

LITE BYTE

?!

It could only be...

*At least a part of the function of melanin in living organisms is to protect them from the malignant effects of UV B rays. Exposure to the rays makes it multiply, mainly to block UV radiation from causing any harm. Of course, there are now super products that prevent UV rays from making any trouble, without the pigment getting ticked off.

NEXT ISSUE
melanin MEETS MATRIMUNIYA

And so, thanks to Supermel and the welcome appearance of Oobtan™, Melanocytee was once again delivered from disrepair and despair.

THE END

melanin
IN
INFINITE
WONDER

DEEPANI SETH

This story started as a piece of nonfiction, based on a day spent with a woman in a small town in eastern India. It was just supposed to be a telling of a part of her day, which could have been any among the several everydays of her life. In the process of writing and illustrating it, the story became something else entirely. The lines between fiction and nonfiction blurred. It became about a woman, in any place, with or without a job, with a home or without one, walking across a city that could have been any city anywhere. Some of it became about my walks around my city, around my many cities.

It is through the telling of the stories of others that we are able to sometimes articulate our own.

I would like to thank my anonymous protagonist for letting me into her life and through it, a part of mine.

I work as a researcher, designer and occasionally an illustrator, chiefly in New Delhi.

Ujjwal Utkarsh, who translated the piece into Hindi, is a film- maker and teaches film-making.

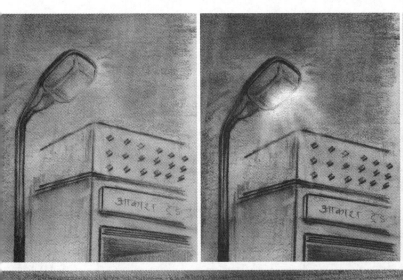

the walk
Deepani Seth

hindi translation:ujjwal utkarsh

सोचो तो हम ढूँढते हैं, और अकसर
पा भी लेते हैं, कुछ रहस्यमई जगह।
कोनें, जो प्रत्यक्ष हैं, पर जिनमें
छुप कर, हम अपने कुछ हिस्सों को
प्रारूप दे सकते हैं। या फिर किसी
और रूप में ढल सकते हैं।

I sometimes think about how we seek – and
often find – secret places in the world,
places where we can hide and, hidden thus,
reveal ourselves, or parts of ourselves,
or become someone else entirely.

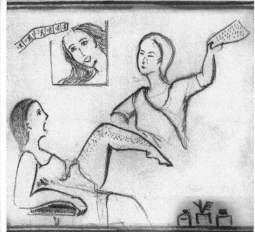

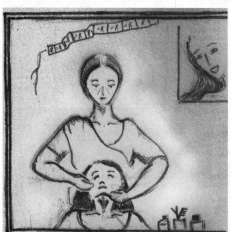

प्री ब्राइडल की
डेट तय कर के
बता देना। बुक
कर दूँगी

Set a date for
the pre-bridal
and let me know.
I'll book it.

अरे अभी तो
इतना कुछ बाकी
है। शादी करना
भी ना एक...

Ah! There's still so
much left to do!
Getting married,
I tell you...

हाँ बॉयफ्रेंड को भी
तो बताना बाकी है...
Yaar. The boyfriend
also has to be informed...

Temporal spaces that we share with other passersby.

Madaaaam!!!

Here comes your boyfriend now!

Doesn't anyone want to recharge their phone today?

Wait, I'll handle this.

This should be fun.

I just thought... maybe... I mean...

What is it?? Is it necessary that one wants to recharge everyday?

Okay, put 25 on my phone. And the special STD calling scheme.

Oh, it's you...

I had asked Soham to get the recharge done, but he must have been busy.

..and sometimes with these passersby we build temporal relationships. Only durations vary.

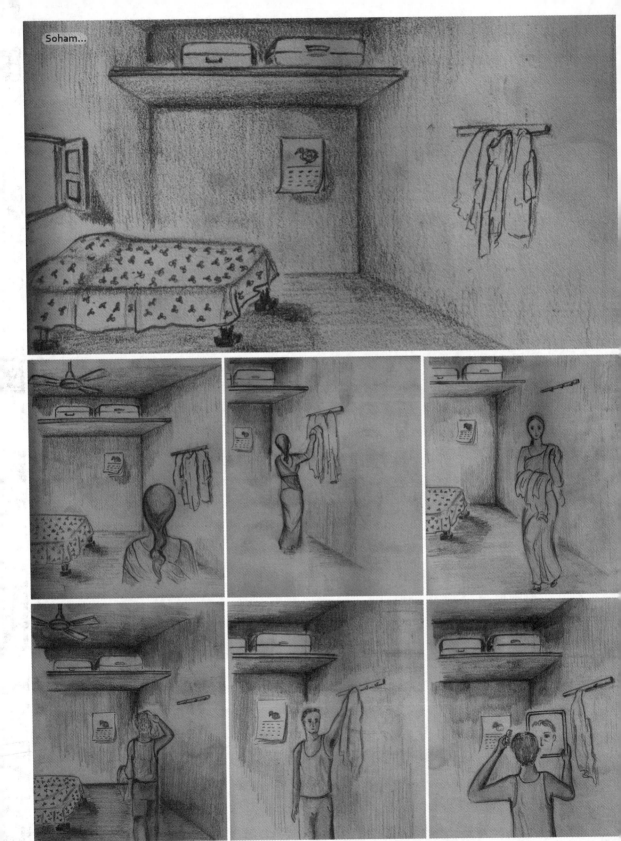

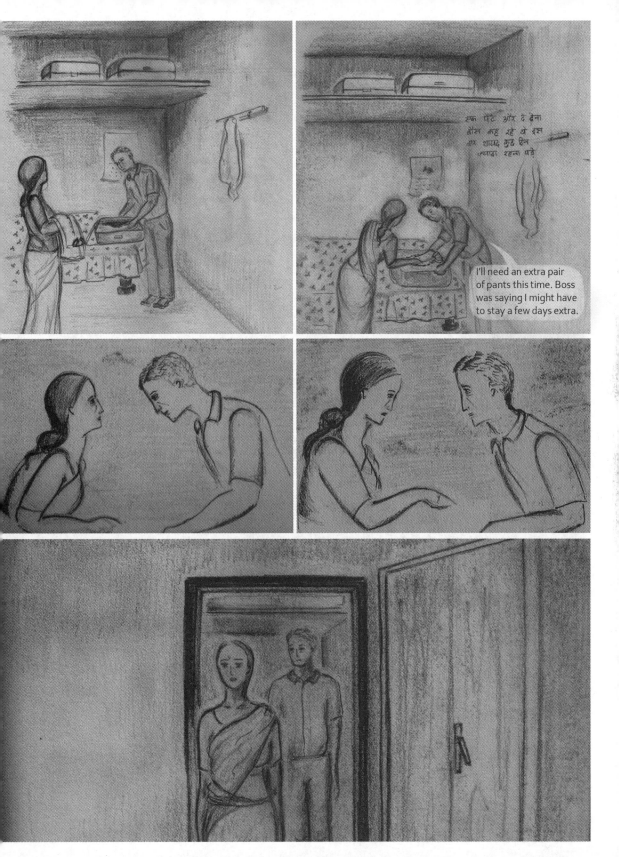

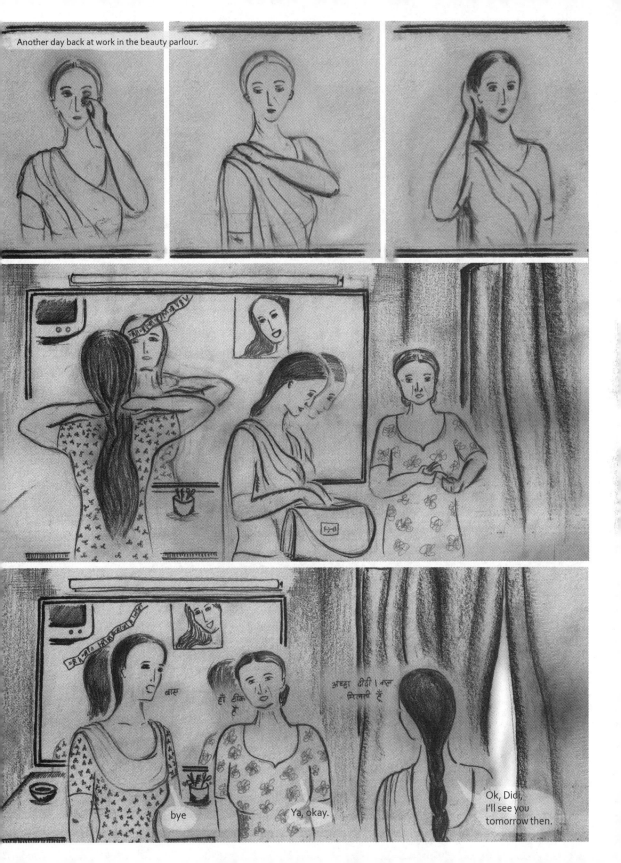

हर दिन कई निगमन, और बहुत सारि अलविदा

Every day
several exits,
several goodbyes.

खो देना , पलों को , जगहों को , पा लेना । खो जाना उन में कभी

Losing spaces, and finding them. Losing oneself, sometimes...

दूसरों की कहानीयों में ढूँढना

Looking into the stories of others

अब खबरें बाहर की दुनिया से

NOW... News from the outside world!!

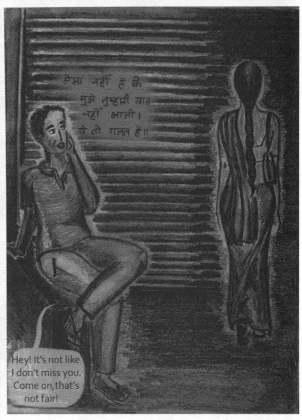

आज चाँद अकेला
है आसमान में

The moon is alone
in the sky today.

एक गहरा खालीपन

Suspended
in a quiet comfortable blankness

समेटे हुए अपने में कितनी अनसुनी कहानियाँ

that holds within it several unheard stories

अगले महीने शहर
जाना पड़ेगा
यहाँ काम मिलना
मुश्किल होता
जा रहा है

I will have to go to the city next month
It's getting difficult to find work here.

अनको रखै हुए

keeping them

जब की उनके रचयता आते जाते हैं
मुसाफ़िरों की तरह
बँजारों की तरह
भटकते हुए।

even as the owners and creators of those stories come and go,
like travellers, like seasonal nomads
moving between temporal spaces

ITA
MEHROTRA

I met with Manipuri activist Irom Sharmila first in New Delhi and then a year later I travelled to Imphal to meet her at the hospital ward of Imphal Central Jail. The little conversation with Sharmila and meeting with other activists for peace in Manipur radically altered my idea of nationhood, struggle, unity and also the body.

Thin and frail, her hair spread across her shoulders, and tucked into a large hospital bed, Sharmila was able to speak with such measured strength and depth of meaning that even back in Delhi, I couldn't stop thinking of her.

I haven't met Sharmila again since then, yet knowing her struggle has shaped the way I think and work in countless ways. Delhi is threatening, and though I feel fear at times, I dare myself to do what I want, when I want. The violence women face in Manipur is brought on largely by the strong presence of the military, who rape and loot at will with the protection of the Armed Forces Special Powers Act.

In Delhi this is not the case, yet women continuously find themselves in spaces where their rights are strongly violated. When I write, draw or take a walk through the city at night, I feel the bond between sisters and across geographies that keeps me going. Sharmila, amongst us, bears the torchlight.

sunanditamehrotra.wordpress.com

The National Daily, Feb 9th 2014: Today a minor girl from Manipur was sexually assaulted in Munirka. She was at her residence in the evening when...

North East Blog: Irom Sharmila enters her 14th year of hunger strike against AFSPA*. Force-fed by a nasal tube in Imphal, now she is...

*The Armed Forces Special Powers Act that applies to some Northeastern states in India and to Jammu and Kashmir, gives the army power to shoot at sight and conduct searches in private homes on grounds of mere suspicion of a person being a terrorist.

It's been four years since I went to meet Sharmila...

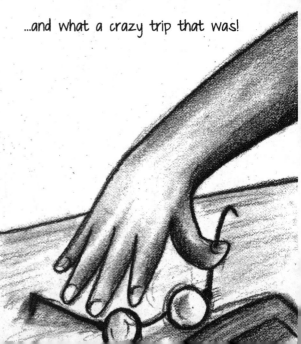

...and what a crazy trip that was!

DELHI IMPHAL
DELHI //////////
23A
1 MAY 2010

INDIGO

As the plane took off, I wondered how Sharmila would be... Weak? Angry? Not wanting to meet outsiders?

From the air Imphal looked like a rice bowl, surrounded by hills.

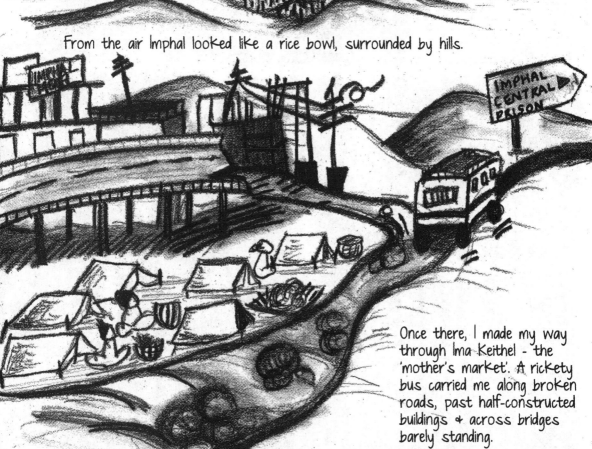

IMPHAL CENTRAL PRISON

Once there, I made my way through Ima Keithel - the 'mother's market'. A rickety bus carried me along broken roads, past half-constructed buildings & across bridges barely standing.

Meet Sharmila??
That's impossible for you!

What group do you represent??

Where do you come from? Show me your documents!

After hours of questions, and with a great deal of suspicion, I was taken to meet Irom.

In the Nupilan war mothers and sisters brandished traditional weapons and were able to hold back the British forces! I am very inspired by her stories...

But even today, it is my sisters who stand up most fiercely against the violence of the army - like they did in the nude protests outside the Kangla camp.

As Sharmila spoke of dreams, food, family and the struggle for peace in Manipur, I realised that she was a young woman first and an activist second. Her choices had indeed made her life different and yet the longing to experience, love and grow was the same. The last thing I expected in the jail ward of Imphal hospital was to make a new friend...

Back in Delhi, I followed Sharmila's story obsessively. Snippets of conversation repeatedly cut through the clutter of exams and work.

And even now, years later, when empty roads are uneasy ways to walk by night,
I think of Sharmila's expanding universe within that one locked room:
as Manipur is hers, Delhi is mine.

Let's ride far out of the city today!

As I write, Irom's silent determination to end army violence in Imphal grows even stronger.

On the 28th of May 2014, she was brought to Delhi to be tried for 'attempt to commit suicide'.

While at the Patiala House court, she said:

'What I was doing was a protest to gain our right to life. I am very eager to live. When they repeal AFSPA, I will eat something, right here, right now.'

HEMAVATHY GUHA

Rape or sexual abuse when committed by a stranger, is often reported by the victim, and she is far more likely to be treated sympathetically. Sexual abuse within the family is far less reported, and a victim of incest is rarely heard and even more rarely gets justice.

Love and respect for elders — as is traditionally expected in India — often stills her voice. Parents fear for their family 'honour', and often dare not take any action against the offending male who enjoys a superior status in the hierarchy with regard to children.

In my story, as is often the case in India, siblings share the same room and usually the same bed, due to lack of space. I have taken the life story of one such girl which is not entirely fictional. Abused by her brother, Asha seeks her father's support. Failing this, she musters the courage to leave home and to build a new life of her own. But the scars remain...

Asha, now

Hemavaty Guha

Asha wakes up with a start. She had felt someone touching her, pinning her down... And yet, there was no one around except her husband who was sleeping peacefully on the other side. It was her recurring nightmare.

As she lies down again, her mind wanders back to her school days...
She is lying on the mattress. She wakes up in the middle of the night. Instinctively, she touches her shirt and finds the buttons open. Her eldest brother is lying beside her, his hand on her breast. Horrified, she pushes him away. She buttons her shirt and turns over.

Asha is taking a shower. Suddenly, the door is pushed open and she sees her brother standing, staring and grinning at her. She screams and shuts the door, weeping with humiliation. Surely, she will complain to father once he comes home.

Asha, older now, is sleeping in the room with her siblings. The nightly visits recur.

Father is no longer there to protect her. Asha contemplates her life and existence. She vows to escape from all this...

Asha shifts to a women's hostel, safe
at last.

She makes new friends, enjoys herself.

Gets married, and a new life begins.

Has Asha got over her past?

She still wakes up with a start in the night – and makes sure she is always there to protect her daughter from her uncle.

KAVERI GOPALAKRISHNAN

Growing up, I could never feel completely comfortable when travelling by public transport or even walking down the street. Like every single teenage girl, I (sometimes unconsciously) adopted different behaviour patterns: dressing differently, changing my body language in public, or trying to blend into my surrounding more to avoid curious or aggressive stares in public.

It was a hot summer afternoon in Delhi that led to a whole day of these conversations with fifteen different women, of various age groups and backgrounds. These, in turn, inspired the questioning, sometimes painfully funny, too-serious mini-comics in 'Basic Space.'

I'm a freelance illustrator and comics artist based in Bangalore. Small personal stories, sketching while travelling and long conversations excite and inspire me. I focus on making work which is both character- and content-driven. The love for sequential narrative comes from growing up reading MAD magazine, and a background in Animation Film Design from the National Institute of Design, Ahmedabad.

kaverigeewhiz.tumblr.com

CHAPTER TWO:
Keeping the LINE, straight everyday

What WOMEN.. WANT?

I asked 18 women, of different ages & from various backgrounds; "WHAT 'LINES' DO YOU DRAW, AS A WOMAN?"

I LOOK DIFFERENT.

IN THE MARKET.

—M, 23.

JUST KEEP A FEW PINS (IN CHENNAI BUSES). MY MOTHER HAS BEEN DOING THIS FOR YEARS.

—S, 51.

STAND—AT—EASE

ATTENTION!

OF COURSE I GO OUT AT NIGHT. WHO CARES? RAPES KEEP HAPPENING! JUST CARRY A DUPATTA FOR AUTO.

CHAPTER 3: Making a BIG CIRCLE (I AM NOT GARBAGE!)

A POPULAR WOMENS' WEBSITE OFFERS THIS HANDY TIP FOR THE AVERAGE, INSECURE TEENAGER: "BEFORE GOING OUT, GIRLS—"

"Imagine—

Your self—

Covered

FROM HEAD TO toes IN A GIANT GARBAGE bag

La la la

NO BODY NOT ONE BODY CAN CROSS THIS BOUNDARY MY BOUNDARY

BUT WAIT! I'M NOT GARBAGE!

AUTO!!!

CHAPTER FOUR:
MY CAT is not ME

MY CAT HAS SOME REAL BOUNDARIES, AND TEACHES ME A LESSON.

IN A COMPLETELY FANTASTICAL SCENARIO; CHAPTER FIVE:

imagine, women.

I ASKED THOSE 18 WOMEN (REMEMBER THEM?) TO IMAGINE A WORLD WHERE "NO ONE WAS LOOKING, OR JUDGING. THESE ARE A FEW OF THE LOUDEST WISHES.

I would not wear ANYthing except a (maybe) flower to accessorise

walk out without DRESSING up like a MAD woman

Run without HUNCHing.

L.IE down KICK BACK in Lodhi gardens in the GRASS. ALONE

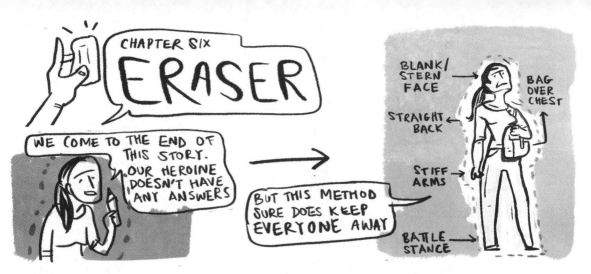

VIDYUN
SABHANEY

I am a writer primarily interested in comics and visual narrative, based in New Delhi. My comics have previously been published by Penguin India, Blaft Publications, and COMIX.INDIA. My research into visual narrative traditions has been supported by India Foundation for the Arts and has been featured in ArtConnect as well as *Sutradhar* and an upcoming issue of *Marg*. I run an independent comics publishing project, Captain Bijli Comics, which aims to develop new content, distribution and dialogue around the form — with two books out and a third on the way.

This particular comic grew out of my research into the pata chitra tradition of Bengal which combines painted scroll and song to tell stories.

BROKEN
LINES

It is difficult for me to keep
track of stories these days.

Having grown up reading books
with a clear beginning, middle
and end, stories without a
resolution just don't stick.

They tear, and begin to merge
hopelessly into one another.

I first noticed this during the media
deluge which followed the
gang-rape of a medical student
in New Delhi in 2012...

Protests erupted; some aimed at amending laws on sexual assault and others just an expression of anger with no goal. Similar incidents began to be reported with greater frequency than before.

Unfinished stories were everywhere

Did you read the article I sent you?

Was it the one in which a woman's fingers were cut off?

What?! No... Where did you read that?

I don't remember...

After getting home that day, I tried to remember where I had read that story. Unsuccessfully. Similar reports were on the front page of every newspaper and magazine in sight. But that particular one was nowhere to be found. I couldn't have imagined it? Could I?

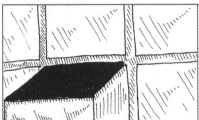

A few days later, I received an email from the editor of a magazine that was publishing an article I had written based on my research into visual-storytelling traditions.

to me ▾

Hi Vidyun:

Hope you are well. Writing in with regard to a caption for the image well. Could you send that information across ASAP?

Thanks

Click here to Reply or Forward

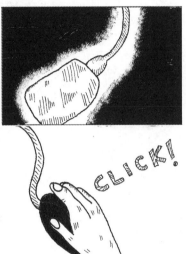

CLICK!

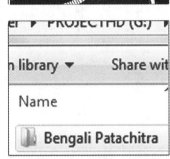

er ▸ PROJECTHD (G:) ▸

n library ▾   Share wit

Name

📁 Bengali Patachitra

OH!

The young woman without fingers was not from a newspaper but from my own archive.

She was a character in a story titled 'Gopalan', which is told in Bhirbhum district of West Bengal as part of the patachitra storytelling tradition.

The mutilation is intended to appease the family's cows, who this young bahu was said to have angered through neglect. It extended to the removal of her knees as well.

A gruesome, cautionary tale for other young bahus in the area.

(Image Source: Arun Patua, Birbhum, West Bengal)

Such warnings are often found in traditional narratives.

Sometimes, they come ensconced in local legend (like Gopalan) and other times they stand out more obviously - for example, gory images that show audiences how they will be punished in Hell for transgression in the temporal realm.

These are most easily found at the end of patas from Bhirbhum. They are recited right at the end of a performance as a warning.

Several of these images bear a striking similarity to punishment described in the *Manusmriti*, both in their didactic tone and violent nature. They range from genital mutilation by rubbing against a khejoor tree for committing adultery, to having one's tongue pierced by a sharp tongs for eating an offering meant for the gods.

The tradition of Bengali patachitra is, however, much wider than narratives of punishment - they tell stories from the Mahabharata, Ramayana, local legend and contemporary events. In the late 19th century, scrolls were even developed to challenge local *zamindars*, in solidarity with the protesting Santhal community. So, it has had a varied and evolving social role.

Pata belonging to Khandu Chitrakar (Naya, West Midnapore)

Because artists are dependent on performances for survival, narratives told in storytelling traditions are often seen to represent ideas that are dominant amongst their audiences and direct patrons.

For example, scrolls on the 9/11 tragedy and the 2004 tsunami are popular because they reflect the concerns of new urban and global audiences.

Their fears, events that shock them or cause them to reflect, acts that give them joy and, sometimes, a strange sense of pleasure.

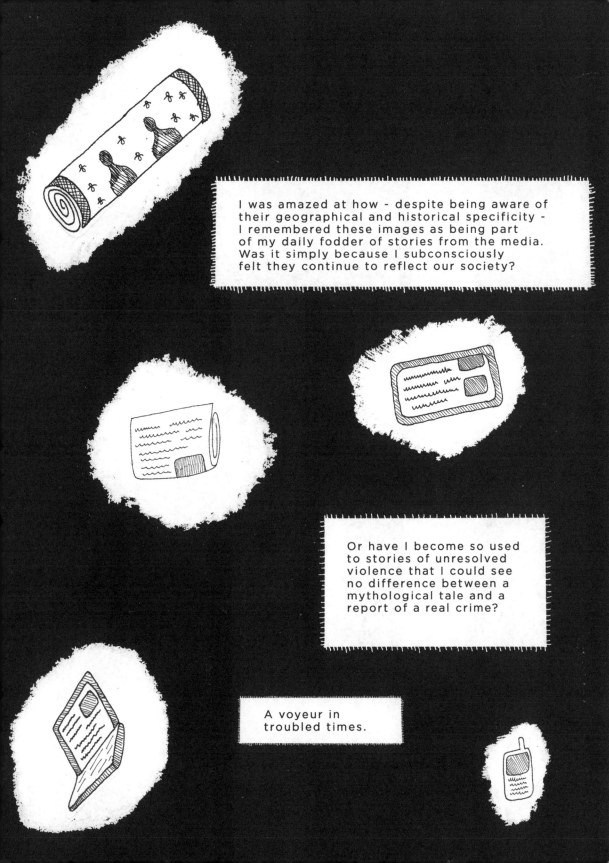

I was amazed at how - despite being aware of their geographical and historical specificity - I remembered these images as being part of my daily fodder of stories from the media. Was it simply because I subconsciously felt they continue to reflect our society?

Or have I become so used to stories of unresolved violence that I could see no difference between a mythological tale and a report of a real crime?

A voyeur in troubled times.

And these broken,
merging lines.

ANGELA
FERRAO

It was always impressed upon us when we were growing up that we should have a good education and a sound trade in hand. This was supposed to equip us for lifelong jobs and financial security. But once I had obtaining all the requisite qualifications, I found that it wasn't so easy to just sail into a job and shop happily ever after.

Every interview threw up different questions, and the goal posts would be shifted. Did it have to do with me being a woman? Of course it did. I noticed that men did not seem to have such problems gaining employment or financial security. Through my short piece, I have tried to focus on some of the issues that women face in their struggle to earn a living with dignity.

I am an illustrator, cartoonist, and writer. I am also the author/illustrator of a children's book titled *Fuloos Plays with the Sun*. I am currently working on my third book for children titled *Fuloos Wins the Race…Almost*.

facebook.com/Ferraodesigns

LADIES PLEASE EXCUSE

WRITTEN AND ILLUSTRATED
BY ANGELA FERRAO

Perennial Search
Your search ends here

Jenny Pinto
Jobs   Qualification

LOOKS LIKE I'M NOT GETTING PAID TODAY EITHER.

Trrrrrr...iiing!

Ding! Dong!

NOW I KNOW WHAT TOOTHPASTE FEELS LIKE!

WE RUN A LARGE ORGANIZATION, NO FIXED TIMINGS, ARE YOU A TEAM PLAYER?

ARE YOU MARRIED? PLANNING TO? NO?

WHAT IF YOU DECIDE TO LEAVE TO GET MARRIED? CAN YOU HANDLE PRESSURE? YOU'RE YOUNG. WE WORK LATE NIGHTS. CAN YOU? SHOULD I HIRE YOU?

I THOUGHT HE WOULD ASK ME ABOUT MY QUALIFICATIONS, EXPLAIN THE JOB... STAY LATE!?! HAS THIS MAN EVER LEFT THE BUILDING?

SURPRISE...

MUMMY! JENNY! SURPRISE! I'VE GOT A GOOD BOSS. HE GAVE ME TIME OFF, AND HERE I AM!

HEY JOHNNY! LOOK AT JOHNNY! GOOD JOB, NO GREAT QUALIFICATIONS. HERE I AM WITH A SLEW OF DEGREES ANSWERING QUESTIONS ABOUT MY OVULATION CYCLE! AND STILL NO JOB.

YOU REALLY THINK I HAVE IT EASY BECAUSE I'M A MAN?

OF COURSE I DO! LOOK AT YOUR QUALIFICATIONS – AND LOOK AT MINE!

YES, BUT I DON'T NEED TO BE ALL THAT QUALIFIED FOR MY JOB.

YOU JUST PROVED MY POINT JOHNNY – YOU HAVE MORE JOB OPTIONS THAN I DO.

SAMIDHA GUNJAL

This is a story about one day, a day unlike any other. The girl in my story has to deal with what is euphemistically called 'eve-teasing' from the men she passes on the street. This kind of sexual harassment is a daily reality for most women in India. Initially she ignores the cat-calls and whistles. Her fear grows but in that moment she finds her strength. Her anger takes over and her emotions explode—she becomes Kali!

Kali is a Hindu goddess associated with Shakti, the force of divine female energy. Kali is the fierce avatar of the goddess Durga who, in need of help, summons Kali to combat demons. Kali is the goddess of Time, Change and Destruction, and is often portrayed as dark and violent.

I am an artist, designer, visual storyteller, illustrator and animator, with an MA in Design in Animation from IDC IIT Bombay. I enjoy drawing cartoons and painting using traditional mediums like pencil, pastels, watercolours and acrylics. As a self-taught artist, I like to experiment with styles and mediums to develop my own style.

samidhag.blogspot.in

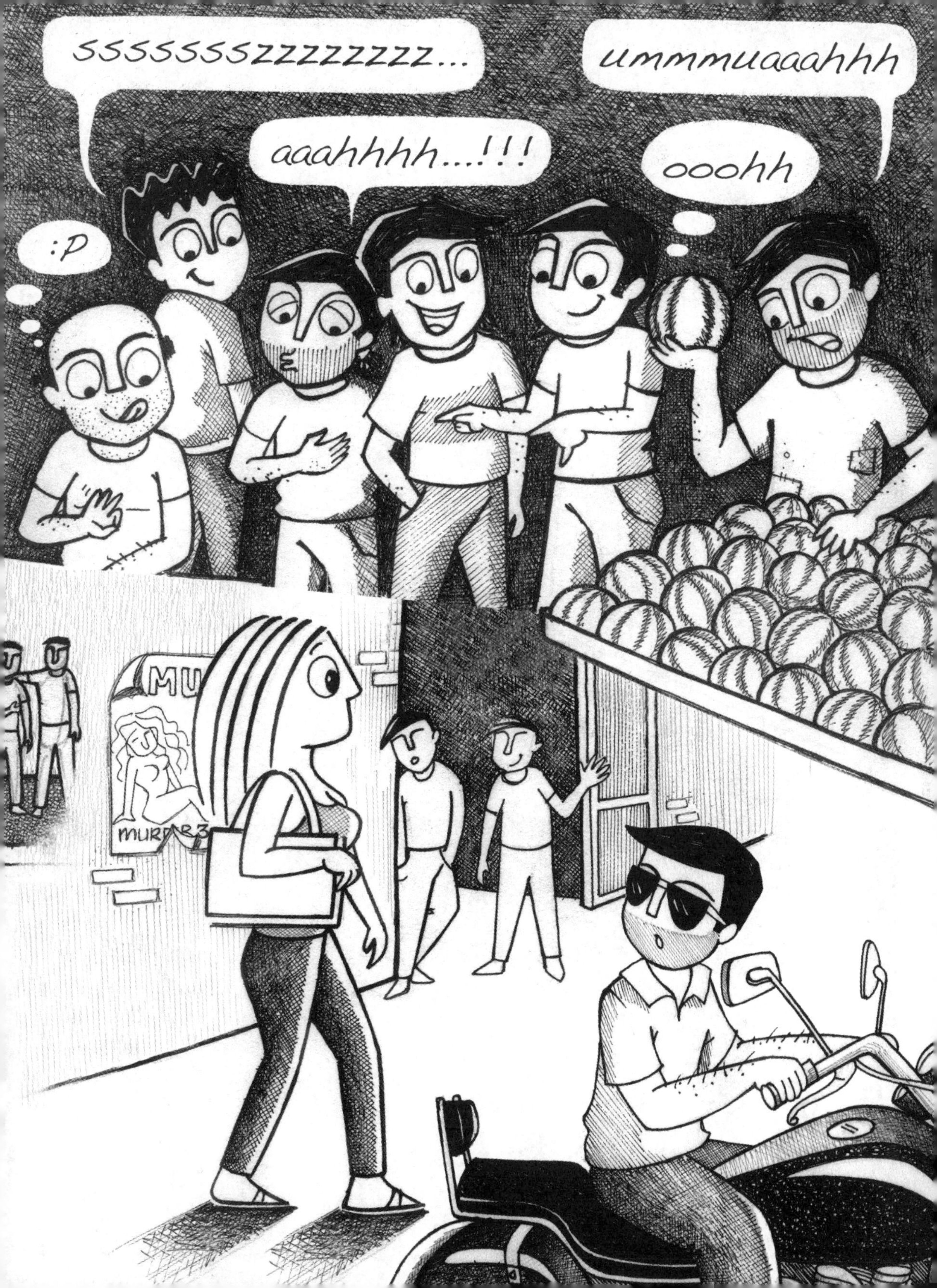

ssssssszzzzzzzz...
:p
aaahhhh...!!!
ooohh
ummmuaaahhh
MU
MURDER3

In April 2014, a group of women graphic artists from across India gathered in the peaceful, green surroundings of Sanskriti Anandgram in New Delhi, ready to embark on an exciting journey. Ludmilla Bartscht and Larissa Bertonasco, two graphic designers making waves in Germany for their politically radical and aesthetically pioneering work, were joined by Priya Kuriyan, one of India's leading illustrators and graphic artists, to head a week-long workshop on graphic storytelling organized jointly by Zubaan Books and Goethe-Institut/Max Mueller Bhavan. The following are their thoughts on the creative process.

PRIYA

To be honest, the idea of mentoring other artists scared me a little. It was the first time I'd been asked to do something like this. What could I offer to the participants that they didn't already know? And, there were the usual anxieties: Would the participants get along or would they want to kill each other by the end of the week? Would the German artists (I had never met Larissa and Ludmilla) and I get along? How would they deal with the slightly chaotic way things usually pan out in India? Day One felt a bit like the first day at college: no one really knew anyone, and everyone was trying to assess the situation they were in. We soon realized that almost none of the participants, apart from one or two, had created comics before. There were also those who were going to be illustrating for the first time. This was going to be challenging! But what was never in doubt was the eagerness and enthusiasm with which they were willing to go for it.

Soon enough, the stories the women wanted to tell tumbled out and the initial reticence vanished. To everyone's relief, it turned out that the group dynamic was electric. Everyone felt free to speak openly and with candour — something that I think was helped by the fact that this was an all-woman group.

At the end of the workshop all of them had with them a basic structure which they

Comics creation workshop, New Delhi, 2014. Photo by Ludmilla Bartscht

would finish up in following months with some online inputs from the three mentors.

There were cultural contexts to many of the stories that often had to be explained to Larissa and Ludmilla and this made me revisit so many plainly bizarre issues that we, as Indian women, have internalized as normal: What is 'eve-teasing'? What does that even mean? Women want to be fairer here? In Germany, people want to get a tan!

India is such a complicated country to describe! The most difficult to explain is that cultures and norms here can change within a matter of a few kilometres. Being a society that is so deeply divided by culture, language and class, yet living in such close proximity with each other, what is considered the norm in one place might not be same in another.

Most of my answers to Larissa's and Ludmilla's queries about cultural aspects of the country — Do Indian women have relationships outside marriage? Is it okay to show artistic images of nude women? — would start with 'It depends…'. In the few days I was with them, I found myself constantly looking at my own country through their eyes with a mixture of amusement, and sometimes a bit of embarrassment. I do think, however, at the end of it, some clichés and stereotypes about Indian women were broken for them, especially after having interacted with this wonderful bunch of women from such diverse backgrounds.

There was something cathartic about all the conversations that we had and to me the real success of the workshop was to see a visible transformation in the confidence of participants; from doubting their abilities to communicate their ideas through comics to actually creating these brave and sparkling stories on their own.

The whole process made me think about my role as a woman in a society that, more often than not, tries to tell you that what you have to say is not important enough. We all have stories to tell, and the difference is really between thinking about it and getting down to actually doing it. In a world that is dominated by stories that are told from male perspectives, I am so thankful for opportunities like this, that help young women storytellers bloom.

LARISSA

Ludmilla Bartscht and I are co-editors and authors of Spring, an annual publication that combines comics, illustration and free drawing in a variety of media. Spring is run by an all-woman collective and, since its inception in 2004, it has become an important network for female artists in Germany.

There, as elsewhere the comics/graphic scene is dominated by men, and we felt that we needed an alternative to counterbalance this. The dynamics and energy changes within an all-female group.

We don't want to write feminist slogans on banners; nor do we want to constantly explain and justify our position.

With this background in mind, we were keen to take up the invitation to help lead a workshop for Indian women artists focussing on gender issues. For us, it was important to not only to broach the issue of violence against women and to reject the narrow view of women as victims, but also to develop a positive and bold outlook. That's why we called the workshop 'Drawing Attention.'

Before Ludmilla and I flew to India, we wondered whether Indian women artists would be so traditional and conservative that we would not be able to talk freely with them about these sensitive topics. One of our friends had warned us not to show any nude drawings of men or women.

What we found on our arrival was an extraordinary group of women who were very frank, curious, full of energy and enthusiasm for drawing, and interested in each other's work.

In the time we spent together, I felt that, in India, it maybe makes even more sense to work only with women. A female group like this provides a protective space where everyone can be who they are and all are treated equally as human beings.

The work we had put into Spring acted as a 'springboard' (excuse the pun!) for 'Drawing Attention'. During the workshop, so many questions were raised that were also running through my mind: Why do so many Indian women wish to lighten their beautiful brown skin? Why, in most parts of India, do women occupy a lower social position than men? Are men, perhaps, afraid of them?

I am convinced that the power of women is always there, within each one of us, and that this is why it is important to reassure each other that there is a way to change the status quo.

I have learned so much during the process of developing this book — perhaps, above all, that we all have common desires and aspirations. And that the only way to realize those desires is by encouraging and helping each other.

Comics creation workshop, New Delhi, 2014.
Photo by Ludmilla Bartscht

LUDMILLA

How can I write about an issue that is so huge with so little space? Is it even possible to tackle emotive subjects without resorting to generalizations and clichés? Whenever I develop a story that is rooted in the real world, a story that is important to me, I have to deal with these kinds of questions.

My last visit to India was over ten years ago, travelling with my boyfriend down the Konkan coast from Mumbai to Kerala. We had our fair share of adventures, but I never felt that I was experiencing life in India truly. Yes, I saw a lot, bought nice things and ate lots of delicious food, but I missed connection one has with people when you are actually working together. I enjoyed my time in India, but didn't particularly want to come back unless it was for a project — something that would provide that connection, bring me together with other people so that we could share each other's lives, thoughts and experiences.

I never expected this to happen, but many years later, it did — and in exactly the way I had wished for.

This background is important, because sometimes things become clearer when you see them in contrast to others. When you want to draw light you need to show the shadow, too. Otherwise the picture will always be partial.

A few years back, I drew a story about sexual abuse. The 'ABC of Tragedy' came out in Spring in 2013 and it caught the eye of Ute Reimer at the Goethe-Institut/Max Mueller Bhavan in India. She already knew one of the other artists in the group (Barbara Yelin), and had been thinking about how to develop a project together.

Somehow my story made her believe that in the Spring collective were the right people to put together a workshop about women's issues with female artists in India.

Both Larissa and I felt that it was very important what the workshop should be called; that it should focus on violence against women but equally would encourage each of the artists to find her own voice in her own special female way. It was not about turning everything on its head or about fighting back using the same awful weapons.

It was about being brave, strong, full of love and goodwill. It was about developing one's own way of being, as a self-determined human being who is respected and loved no matter what your gender.

Men and women don't have to be the same — they are not — but they should have the same resources and the same possibilities to make their own decisions in life.

The Drawing Attention workshop was wonderful. I loved the atmosphere, the warmth between the participants, the paradise-like-garden we were living in, the food.... And, above all, to see how much this encouraged the young women to continue developing their work, to stick to what they were doing. It means a lot to have been a part of something that went on without us and still does.

The workshop would not have been so wonderful if it weren't for all the fantastic participants. For their willingness to share and work together, and for being so open, generous, funny and smart — thank you!

NICOLE

Here in North America, it was around the time of DTL's release in India that we first heard about the project. As the founder of Ad Astra Comix, Drawing the Line: Indian Women Fight Back! was just the comic I'd been looking for: strong, accessible, and amplifying the voices of women I rarely hear from in the media, let alone in comics, my medium of choice.

It quickly became clear that our little Toronto-based comics company would need to step up to the plate if we wanted to do a North American edition of this title some justice! Here was a book we not only wanted to publish and promote; Drawing the Line reflected a collective creative process that we wanted --indeed, had been planning, wishing, hoping-- to emulate in some comics creation workshops of our own.

That opportunity came around the time that we prepared to launch our pre-order campaign for the book. I had been in conversation with the youth group of the Afghan Women's Organization in Mississauga, ON (for anyone not in our area, that's the city directly west of Toronto). Here, Drawing the Line is becoming a powerful comics-creating tool.

These teens, as exhausted as they are by homework and pestering little brothers, have important things to say, to themselves and the world at large.

School assignments and family obligations aside, when will they find the time to have those important moments for reflection and expression?

Time to sort out the complexity of migration, of race, religion, culture, identity, in a country like Canada where they are considered a "minority" on all accounts?

Time to consider what it means to be a woman living between all of these intersections, amid all the noise of mainstream media pressuring us to be, as Soni Singh suggests, an "ideal woman"?

As a white woman leading a workshop with young women of colour, I fit the bill of being a feminist that can do more harm than good if I don't check my privilege in such a situation. That's why Drawing the Line and other comics that reflect women of colour and international voices are so valuable.

As Drawing the Line goes to print, we are continuing our weekly workshop series, and the results have been eye-opening.

Consider the idea that, across this continent, young people are struggling with racism, sexism, Islamophobia, homophobia, transphobia, abuse and mental illness at a time when there is precious little space in educational settings to learn emotional self-defense. Let comics be a refuge. Give them the space to imagine. You, in turn, will discover how much young people have to teach us.

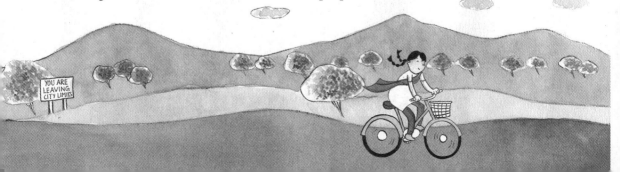

YOU ARE
LEAVING
CITY LIMITS

the panel is political.

If you are a fan of seeing comics that can talk about social justice, Ad Astra Comix would like to keep in touch! We specialize in comics that promote marginalized voices, and work to dismantle oppressive frameworks. Look for us online!

website	adastracomix.com
facebook	facebook.com/adastracomix
twitter	twitter.com/adastracomics
instagram	instagram.com/adastracomix
tumblr	adastracomix.tumblr.com
pinterest	pinterest.com/adastracomix
e-mail	adastracomix@gmail.com

THANK YOU TO ALL OF OUR KICKSTARTER SUPPORTERS!
YOU MADE THIS BOOK POSSIBLE!